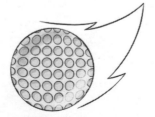

To Lee McAlpine and the endless golf balls
he's lost in the pursuit of par-fection.
C.G.

For all the kids in the world, this is just
a peek at the amazing things you can do.
L.A.

Written by Clive Gifford
Illustrations by Lu Andrade

First published in Great Britain 2024 by Red Shed, part of Farshore

An imprint of HarperCollins*Publishers*
1 London Bridge Street, London SE1 9GF
www.farshore.co.uk

HarperCollins*Publishers*
Macken House, 39/40 Mayor Street Upper,
Dublin 1, D01 C9W8

Copyright © HarperCollins*Publishers* Limited 2024

ISBN 978 0 00 860611 4
Printed and bound in the UK using 100% Renewable Electricity at CPI Group (UK) Ltd.
001

A CIP catalogue record for this title is available from the British Library.

MIX
Paper | Supporting
responsible forestry
FSC™ C007454

This book contains FSC™ certified paper and other controlled
sources to ensure responsible forest management.

For more information visit: www.harpercollins.co.uk/green

INCREDIBLE
GOLF

Written by Clive Gifford
Illustrations by Lu Andrade

RED■
SHED

"Golf is deceptively simple
and endlessly complicated.
It is at the same time rewarding
and maddening – and is without
a doubt the greatest game
humankind has ever invented."

– seven-time major winner
Arnold Palmer

Contents

Introduction

Welcome to the extraordinary game of golf! From crunching drives to delicate putts, this sport is one of the few that *anyone* can play. No matter whether you're seven or seventy years old, you can head out onto the course and enjoy a round with your friends. And far from being a stuffy sport, golf can be tense, dramatic and exciting to watch or play. You need skill, strength and ice-cold nerves to shoot as low a score as you can.

On these pages you'll find tons of amazing facts, feats and stories about the world of golf and the many extraordinary people who have played it. From Rory McIlroy to the Ryder Cup, exploding golf balls to sharks in water hazards, and hippos in the rough to golf shots in space, this book has it all!

Want to know which golf hole you'll need a helicopter to play? Or the tournament you can only participate in if you're dressed as Santa Claus? Well, turn the pages to find out!

The language of golf is packed full of strange terms like 'dogleg' and 'bogey', but we've got you covered with a glossary on pages 160–164. There's also a section on the basics of playing golf and a quiz to challenge your golfing knowledge. So, let's tee off and enjoy a round . . . of reading.

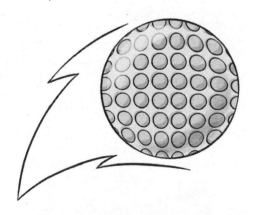

"I love golf. I love every single part of it."
– two-time major winner Collin Morikawa

Banned!

Golf is one of the oldest sports around. It stretches back hundreds of years. In 1457, for example, Scottish ruler King James II made a new law banning golf. Eek! The reason? King James had discovered that many of his subjects were playing golf instead of improving their archery skills, and he was worried that he'd lose his next battle if his archers were out of practice.

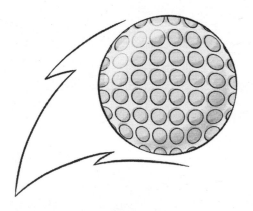

Here We Go Again

The next two kings of Scotland, James III and James IV, (James as a king's name was all the rage at the time) also banned the game. The King after them, James V, had a change of heart. After he'd signed a treaty in 1502 with England, he thought fighting was less likely to happen. King James felt that archery was no longer as crucial to his kingdom's safety, so he unbanned golf. Hurrah! He also paid a craftsman in Perth to make him a set of 'clubs' at a cost of 14 shillings (about £465 in today's money, which would have bought you a cow!).

Golf Ball Meteor

During a six-hour spacewalk in 2006 at the International Space Station (ISS), Russian cosmonaut Mikhail Tyurin whipped out a gold-plated 6-iron golf club and played a historic shot. He struck a specially-made golf ball, weighing only 3 g, into space. No need to cry 'Fore!'.

DID YOU KNOW?

Golf has a bird-brained unofficial scoring system. 'Par' is the number of shots an expert golfer is expected to complete a hole in. One under par is called 'a birdie', two under par is 'an eagle' and three under par is 'an albatross'.

Mikhail and the ISS were over 400km above the Pacific Ocean at the time of his shot. Scientists estimate the ball travelled at least two million kilometres before burning up in the Earth's atmosphere. This makes it the longest shot ever played.

DID YOU KNOW?

In 2021, South Korean golfer Sungjae Im scored his 494th birdie of the season – incredible! This is a Professional Golfers' Association (PGA) Tour record since birdie statistics were first kept.

Clinical Patty

American Patty Berg was one of women's golf's first professional superstars. She was the first president of the Ladies Professional Golf Association (LPGA) and won more than 60 titles – including an incredible 15 majors, which is still a record in women's golf.

What made her impact on the game even more remarkable was the fact she played over 16,000 golf clinics during her career to encourage women and men to take up the sport. Patty racked up hundreds of thousands of kilometres criss-crossing America, helping to turn golf into the popular pastime it is now.

Father and Son

Men and women's golf both have their biggest, most highly-prized tournaments. They're known as the 'majors'. For men, the majors start with the Masters at Augusta in April, then the PGA Championship in May, the US Open in June, before top golfers cross the Atlantic and compete in the Open Championship in the UK or Ireland in July. Winning any of these events nowadays would earn you a cool £2 million or more. Not bad for four rounds of golf!

Yet when the first major was played all the way back in 1860, the winner only received the loan of a leather belt reckoned to be worth £25! You had to win the tournament three times to take ownership of the belt. The Open Championship was the first major and attracted just eight golfers. They played three rounds of a 12-hole golf course in Prestwick, Scotland. Willie Park Senior won the prize. Second place went to Old Tom Morris who roared back to win two years later by 13 shots, still the biggest margin of victory at the tournament.

Prize money was introduced in 1867, when Old Tom won his fourth Open. He won £7 (around £1000 these days) at the age of 46 – making him the oldest winner to this day. The following year, his son, Young Tom Morris, won the first of four Opens in a row, becoming the youngest ever men's major winner at the tender age of 17.

One-Handed Golfer

Most professional golf tournaments are played over four rounds. After two rounds the number of competitors is reduced: those with the highest scores are out of the competition. Players still in the competition are said to have made the cut. They're often the golfers most on form and playing well.

In the 1974 Tallahassee Open, American pro golfer Mike Reasor made the cut with a score of 144 after two rounds on the Killearn Country Club course. To earn qualification for the next PGA Tour event – the Byron Nelson Classic – the following week, Mike needed to complete the next two rounds to finish the tournament. Making the cut wasn't unusual for Mike (he made cuts at over 100 PGA Tour tournaments during his career), but falling off a friend's horse that evening certainly was! Mike dislocated his left shoulder, injured his knee and tore rib cartilage.

Ow, ow, OW!

The following day, despite the pain, he was still intent on qualifying for the next tournament. So he played the course by swinging his 5-iron one-handed and tucking the hand of his injured arm inside his belt. Mike completed his third round in 123 shots: 51 shots over par. Ouch!

"**Word had gotten around the course what this crazy fool was doing. We had more people watching us than the leaders.**"

– Mike Reasor

Whilst any hope of victory had long gone, Mike battled on to complete the tournament. Large crowds cheered him on near the end of the fourth and final round where he carded a slightly improved 114. That meant he completed the tournament and qualified for the next, but with possibly the highest score in professional golf – 93 over par. Unfortunately, Mike's injuries prevented him from playing the following week.

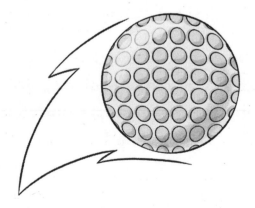

Fishy Business

Women were playing golf in Scotland 400–500 years ago, but the first women's tournament we know about didn't start until 1811. It was held in Musselburgh and only the wives of local fishermen could take part!

Although we don't know the names of the competitors who came first and second, we do know that the winner received a fishing basket and a shawl, and the runner-up was given two silk handkerchiefs from Spain.

Big Drive

Driving ranges are great places to practise your golf shots. You pay for a bucket of balls that you can hit down a range without worrying about having to collect them afterwards. The largest range in the world is the SKY72 Dream Golf Range in Incheon, South Korea, where up to 300 golfers can practise at the same time.

DID YOU KNOW?

Until the early 20th century golf clubs weren't numbered like irons and woods are today. Instead they had unusual names such as 'mashies' (similar to a 5-iron), 'niblicks' (like a 9-iron) and 'brassies' (similar to a 2-wood).

Breaking Sixty

Sometimes, everything goes right for a pro golfer on a round. They may be scoring birdie after birdie on the holes and are well under par for their round. But can they keep it going to join an elite group of less than 12 golfers who've completed 18 holes in less than 60 shots?

Al Geiberger was the first to do it on the PGA Tour in 1977 with an eagle and 11 birdies on a par 72 course. As Al's other rounds in the tournament were 72, 72 and 70, he managed to win the event without a single one of his rounds being in the 60s – very unusual.

Jim Furyk finished his second round at the 2013 BMW Championship in 59. Three years later, he went one better, scoring a 58 at the Travelers Championship.

Amazingly, Jim missed three good chances to go even lower – a 55 would have been CRAZY! He's still the only player to have broken 60 twice on the PGA Tour.

In women's golf, only one player has hit the landmark on the LPGA Tour, and that's the great Annika Sörenstam in 2001. She set off for her second round at the Standard Register Ping tournament in

DID YOU KNOW?

The impact between the golf club and ball lasts less than one thousandth of a second. Golf ball manufacturers strive to make that tiny amount of time count by spending fortunes on research using wind tunnels and supercomputers. They even use robots to swing clubs and strike balls in precisely the same way over and over again.

a threesome that included her sister, Charlotta, who was the event's defending champion. Annika blazed eight birdies in the first eight holes, completed the ninth hole in par, then added a further five birdies to score an incredible 13-under-par round of 59.

"When I do a clinic and we talk about being positive, I bring up the 59 and make girls believe what can happen. The ball doesn't know who you are, so just keep going!"

– Annika Sörenstam

DID YOU KNOW?

A golf ball's surface is covered in hundreds of crater-like dimples. These help create lift, reduce drag and allow the ball to travel further than if it was smooth. All balls have to be at least 42.67mm in diameter and must weigh less than 45.93g.

The Old Course

The oldest golf course is near Scotland and is open to the public. In 1552, Archbishop John Hamilton was given permission to use land by the sea at St Andrews to breed rabbits. This permission, written in a charter (a type of contract), also confirmed the rights of local people to play golf on the land.

By the 1750s, the 12-hole Royal and Ancient Golf Club had been founded at St Andrews. A round was 22 holes, so ten of the holes were played twice. Some of the holes were later considered too short, so were combined. New holes were built until the Old Course, as it became known, featured 18 holes.

> **"I fell in love with it the first day I played it. There's just no other golf course that is even remotely close."**
>
> – Jack Nicklaus

The course has barely changed in the last 125 years and includes 112 devilishly deep, steep and difficult sand traps with names like 'the Beardies', 'the Coffins' and 'Hell Bunker'. Fourteen of the course's 18 holes share greens, meaning there are two pins and flags on each green. Make sure you aim for the right one!

Winning Whitworth

Kathy Whitworth won a record 88 LPGA tournaments during her career – more than any other player. It could have been many more, but Kathy had a poor record in play-offs (used to separate two or more players tied on the final score). In the 28 play-offs she contested, Kathy only won eight.

Christmas Play

Every December, the Kris Kringle Open competition
is held at the Upper Montclair Country Club course
in New Jersey, USA. More than 150 competitors play
the tournament, and they all dress up in full Father
Christmas outfits! All the profits go to local charities.

Young Guns

Many golfers start young but few have had success so early as this trio of young guns.

In 1989, Thuashni Selvaratnam won the Sri Lanka Amateur Golf Championship. She was only 12 years old, making her the youngest player to win a national title. In 1967, Beverly Klass qualified to play in the US Women's Open. She was only ten years, seven months and 21 days old! It would be another nine years before she joined the LPGA Tour.

In 2013, Tianlang Guan from China qualified to play in the Masters at Augusta. The 14 year old played all four rounds, making him the youngest player to make the cut at a major championship.

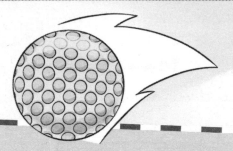

Brilliant Babe

Name: Babe Didrikson Zaharias

Born: 1911

Died: 1956

Country: USA

Professional tournament wins: 48

Major wins: 10

Super stat: Won 20 tournaments in the fastest time ever (two years, four months).

Famous for: Being a multi-talented sportsperson who pioneered powerful, athletic women's golf

Mildred 'Babe' Didrikson Zaharias was an incredible sportswoman from America. From baseball to tennis to volleyball, she excelled at every sport she attempted. Fresh out of high school, she joined a championship-winning ladies basketball team and competed in athletics. In fact, she turned up at the 1932 Women's Amateur Athletic Union (AAU) Championships as a one-woman team, took part in eight events, and won the entire competition.

Later that year, Babe struck gold twice, silver once and broke a world record in the 100m hurdles during the Olympics. She is the only Olympic athlete – male or female – to win medals in running (hurdles), throwing (javelin) and jumping (high jump) events.

Babe's attention turned to golf in 1933 and it wasn't long before she tasted big tournament success, winning the Texas Women's Amateur Championship in 1935. Despite being relatively small, Babe developed a powerful swing and drove the ball farther than other female players of the time.

"It's not just enough to swing at the ball. You've got to loosen your girdle and really let the ball have it!"
– 'Babe' Didrikson Zaharias

After the Second World War, Babe dominated amateur golf. In the 1946 and 1947 seasons, she won an incredible 17 tournaments in a row. She turned professional and won the first of ten majors in 1948, the same year that she qualified to play in the men's US Open. However, she was refused admission. Boo!

1950 proved to be her greatest year. She won eight tournaments, including all three of the women's majors at the time. In total, Babe won 41 events on the Ladies Professional Golf Association (LPGA) tour. She changed women's golf, which was no longer seen as a gentle game, but an athletic sport requiring power and skill.

Skimming Shot

Spanish golfer Jon Rahm was practising for the 2020 Masters tournament when he reached the 16th hole of the Augusta National Course in America. In competition, players normally send their ball high to clear the enormous stretch of water that stands between the tee and the green. Jon chose a different route and hit the ball low so it skipped across the water – just like you'd skim a pebble across the sea! His ball popped up onto the green and slowly rolled round its contours but it couldn't roll into the hole, could it?

It could!

Incredibly, it was Jon's second hole-in-one during practice for the tournament; he'd bagged one the day before. And he started the tournament hot, becoming joint leader after two rounds before finishing in a tie for seventh.

In 2020, Jon became only the second World Number One golfer from Spain (after Seve Ballesteros). And the following year, he became the first Spanish golfer to win the US Open – his first major. Unlike his rapid start in practice before the 2020 Masters, he didn't lead the field of the tournament until the 71st hole of the 72-hole competition.

Cross-country Course

The sixth hole of the Tornio / Meri-Lapin golf course sits on the border between Finland and Sweden, meaning you get to play one round in two countries. What makes it more fun is that Finland and Sweden are in different time zones, so you have to adjust your watch by an hour when playing the sixth!

DID YOU KNOW?

The Riviera golf course in Los Angeles, USA has a deep bunker placed right in the middle of the green. Players have to putt carefully around it – you don't want to fall into that sand trap.

A New Way to Play

Clint Russell was a keen amateur golfer who lost his eyesight in 1924 during a fire. Undeterred, Clint decided to teach himself how to play by using a caddie to tee up his ball, adjust his stance and line up his club face to the target. Clint worked hard and in 1930 shot an amazing round of 84. Eight years later, he played a match against a severely visually impaired English doctor, William 'Beach' Oxenham, which was billed as the world championship of blind golf.

Clint won. But more importantly the match attracted a lot of spectators and press interest. Soon, other visually impaired golfers were playing, using a caddie or assistant to guide them round the course. Associations in the USA and elsewhere sprang up to assist visually impaired people on their journey into golf and to arrange tournaments for them to compete in.

One of the biggest tournaments is the Vision Cup where a North American team play a Rest of the World team in a similar fashion to the Ryder or Solheim Cup. The 2022 edition was held at the famous TPC Sawgrass course and saw North America triumph for the first time in five tournaments.

At big tournaments, the golfers compete in three different categories: B1 for those who are blind, B2 for those with five per cent sight and B3 for those with ten per cent sight. At ten per cent, you can see the ball and some shapes as a blur.

DID YOU KNOW?

The first official women's golf club was founded at St Andrews in 1867. The Ladies Putting Club played on a large and hilly putting green built by famous golfer and greenkeeper Old Tom Morris. It was nicknamed the 'Himalayas' for its up-and-down play. The large, heavy dresses of the day made it harder for women to complete a full swing. Women were not allowed to play on the Old Course, and it wasn't until 1903 that women golfers got to compete there with the Scottish Ladies Championship.

Fin-essing the Ball

Carbrook Golf Club in Brisbane, Australia, has a little something extra in its water hazards to worry golfers – sharks! The bull sharks, some of which are three metres long, reached the course's central lake years ago when a nearby river broke its banks and flooded. Golfers who hit their ball into the lake don't go looking for it because bull sharks do sometimes attack and bite humans!

Having a Ball

It's thought that golf balls used in the 15th and 16th centuries were probably roughly carved spheres made from hardwood such as beech. It would be pretty hard to hit them very far, and experts believe 60–80m would have been the maximum. Dutch craftspeople invented the 'hairy ball' in the 1500s. These were small leather sacks stuffed with cow's hair or straw.

In 1618, the 'featherie ball' was developed. It was a leather pouch packed full of goose or chicken feathers and assembled when wet. As it dried out, the feathers and pouch shrunk to form a small, hard, roundish ball. The featherie flew further than the hairy and wooden balls, but they were expensive to make and could split on landing. They also got heavier when wet, which made them tougher to hit.

A better ball was needed, and in the 19th century,
rubbery sap from a Malaysian tree helped make that
happen. According to legend, the first 'gutta percha'
ball made with rubber was developed by Scottish
clergyman Reverend Dr Robert Adams in 1848. Gutta
percha balls were cheaper, more durable and could
be hit hard. As swings increased in power, some
golfers began wrapping the top of their wooden golf
club shafts with leather to cushion the impact – and so
the golf club grip was born!

The next big jump in golf ball technology came in 1898 when American sportsman Coburn Haskell experimented with winding rubber thread (a bit like a long, thin elastic band) around a core made of solid rubber. When encased in a tough outer skin of gutta percha, the Haskell ball flew and bounced really well.

There have been lots of improvements to golf balls since then. Huge amounts of research go into perfecting balls that fly further or are easier to hit. After all, it's a big business that sells an incredible 1.2 billion balls every year.

Drop Zone

In 1928, a game of aerial golf was played by aviators flying above the Westbury Golf Club in New York. Competitors flew over the course and dropped golf balls. The winner was the one who got their ball closest to the hole.

DID YOU KNOW?

Famous American actor Samuel L. Jackson loves golf so much he includes it in his movie contracts. A key condition of him appearing in a movie is that he can play golf twice a week during filming!

Extreme 19

One of the strangest holes in golf is found at the Legend Golf & Safari Resort in South Africa. The Extreme 19th tee is on Hanglip Mountain, 400m above the green, and is shaped like the African continent. Balls takes 20 seconds to land after the drive! And that's not the strangest thing: to play the hole, you need to ride a helicopter to and from the tee.

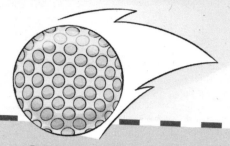

Pioneering Player

Name: Althea Gibson

Born: 1927

Died: 2003

Country: USA

Professional tournament wins: 0

Major wins: 0

Super stat: Five years in the LPGA's top 50 money winners list

Famous for: A world-class tennis player who became the first African-American to join the LPGA Tour

Althea Gibson was an African-American tennis star who won the French Open and twice won Wimbledon and the US Open in the 1950s. In the 1960s, aged 36, she switched to golf and became the first African-American to join the LPGA professional tour.

Although the players welcomed Althea, some of the golf clubs who hosted the tournaments did not. Some hotels discriminated against her by refusing to let her stay, and some courses wouldn't even let her use their changing rooms. Althea often had to endure racist abuse as she played her shots. During one event, Althea wasn't allowed into the course clubhouse, so she had to change into her golf gear in her car. When her fellow golfers discovered this, they showed their support by also changing in their cars.

Although she never won an LPGA tournament, she got close by coming second in a 1970 event and winning a car at another. She played in 171 LPGA competitions and was a popular member of the tour before retiring in the late 1970s as a true pioneer of diversity in sport.

Superstitions

Many golfers are superstitious. They may have a lucky ball, club or pair of socks they like to use or wear to give them good fortune, or something they must avoid to keep bad luck at bay.

Even top golfers have good-luck charms and superstitions. The great American Jack Nicklaus believed that three was a lucky number and would always play with three coins in his pocket. English pro golfer Holly Clyburn thinks the number four is unlucky and won't play with golf balls with that number on them. American Lee Trevino believed yellow golf tees were unlucky, so he never touched them.

South African legend Ernie Els is nicknamed the Big Easy for his low-key, unflappable manner on and off the course. Surprisingly, he is superstitious and will not use a golf ball after he has scored a birdie or eagle with it. The reason? He believes that the ball has used up its luck and has to be replaced with a fresh one.

Some superstitions surround players' clothing, such as Tiger Woods' red shirt (see p71). Young English professional Sophie Keech always goes out onto the course wearing odd socks. Another female pro, Paula Creamer, earned the nickname the Pink Panther for her habit of wearing an all-pink outfit for the last round of any tournament she competes in.

Other players are superstitious about the ball marker they use on the green. A marker allows them to take their ball away for a clean or because it's in the path of another player's putt. Former world number one Dustin Johnson always uses a US quarter (a coin worth 25 cents) as his ball marker. He insists the coin must be dated from some time in the 1960s. For Christina Kim, her superstition lies on the edge of the green where it meets the fairway. She adjusts her stride so she never steps on that border, which she believes would be bad luck!

DID YOU KNOW?

Spanish restaurant owner Robert Lantsoght has amassed the world's biggest collection of golf clubs. An incredible 4,393 golf clubs can be found at his restaurant in the Costa del Sol, most hanging from the ceiling!

Ice Is Nice

Every winter in Siberia, Russia hardy competitors
put on their thermal underwear and warm parkas
to compete in the Baikal Prize Open. This golf
tournament is played over nine holes on the iced-
over surface of Lake Baikal, the world's deepest lake.
Players use brightly-coloured red, orange and yellow
balls and must avoid hazards like bunkers filled with
snow. They must also contend with the super-fast 'greens'
made of smoothed ice that their ball will quickly skate
across if struck too hard.

Fore!

No one is certain who first shouted 'FORE!' to warn people about a flying golf ball heading towards them. We know it was in use in the 19th century and one theory comes from the cost of golf balls in the sport's early days. Because they were hand-made, early golf balls were very expensive, so some golfers employed people to stand further up the hole, roughly where their ball would land. The aim was to reduce the number of lost balls. These people were called forecaddies and a cry of 'Forecaddie!', later shortened to "Fore!", may have been used to get their attention.

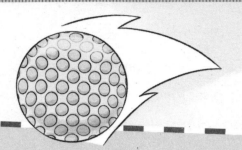

Straight as an Arrow

Name: Calvin Peete

Born: 1943

Died: 2015

Country: USA

Professional tournament wins: 14

Major wins: 0

Super stat: In 1,200 rounds of golf, Calvin only hit the ball out of bounds *once*!

Famous for: Self-taught, extremely accurate player who became the most successful Black golfer on the PGA tour before Tiger Woods

American Calvin Peete grew up one of nineteen children in a poor family. When he was 12, he fell out of a tree and broke his elbow. The bone wasn't set properly and left him with a bent arm for the rest of his life.

Calvin didn't even pick up a golf club until he was 23 years old and never took a golf lesson.

He was 32 when he turned professional in 1975, but made up for lost time, becoming the most successful African-American player of his era.

He won 12 PGA tournaments and had 72 top-ten finishes. Despite his disability, he was the PGA Tour leader for driving accuracy, not for one or two seasons, but for ten in a row (1981–1990).

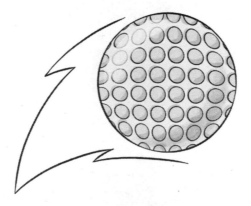

Oh, Brother!

Married couple Vitale and Anna Turnesa emigrated from Italy to the United States in 1904. Vitale worked first in construction then as a greenkeeper at the Fairview Country Club. The pair had seven sons, six of whom – Mike, Doug, Jim, Phil, Frank and Joe – all became professional golfers. Jim Turnesa won the 1952 PGA Championship whilst Joe finished second twice in major championships. The seventh brother, Willie, didn't turn pro but was still a talented golfer who won the British Amateur Championship in 1947 and the US Amateur the following year!

Better Than a Birdie

A 'condor' is the name given to making a four under par score on a single hole. This usually means you have made a hole-in-one on a par five – almost impossible. On some golf courses, there are ultra-long par-six holes. So, you could get a condor by completing these holes in two shots. Also, almost impossible.

The first time it was known to have occurred was in 1962. American golfer Larry Bruce was playing at the Hope Country Club in Arkansas. He stood on the fifth tee, let rip with his drive and watched his ball sail over a big stand of trees and right into the hole, 480 yards (439m) away. What a shot!

The most recent condor moment was in 2020 when ten-handicap golfer, Kevin Pon, hit an astonishing drive at the Lake Chabot course in California. Kevin was playing the formidable 649-yard 18th on the course – a rare par-six hole. His drive bounced off a hard tarmac path, gaining extra distance, before rolling downhill to finish 550 yards from the tee. Kevin couldn't believe it, and yet his next shot was even better... The ball pitched, bounced several times, then rolled into the cup. Awesome! Kevin's condor made the local TV news and months later, people were still coming up to him asking for his autograph.

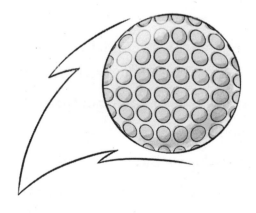

Caddie Chaos

The word 'caddie' may have come from Mary, Queen of Scots (1542–1587 CE), almost 500 years ago. She is said to have called some of her servants 'cadet' or 'caddies'. Caddying is often a way for enthusiastic junior golfers to earn some money and gain experience. At professional level, top caddies can earn a really good living, especially if their player wins tournaments, as they receive a portion of the prize money.

Caddies don't just carry the bag (which fully-loaded can weigh over 20kg). They also look after the golfer's clubs and other equipment, assess distances and conditions on each hole, prepare notes for their golfer, and more besides. Occasionally, even top caddies let their golfer down. Here are three examples of caddie chaos!

In 1979, Mark Freiburg was caddying for American golfer Curtis Strange at a PGA tournament in Florida. As he carried the bag over a bridge to the ninth hole, he slipped, tilted the bag and more than half the clubs fell into the water below. Curtis had to continue his round with just four clubs – three irons and his putter. The clubs were recovered by a diver later that day!

At the 2006 Ryder Cup, Steve Williams, Tiger Woods' long–time caddie, was leaning on Tiger's 9-iron when the club slipped and fell into the water. The caddie couldn't retrieve it and didn't dare tell his golfer. Steve hoped that Tiger wouldn't ask for that club on the last part of the round, but on the very next hole Tiger requested his 9-iron. Steve had to fess up, but apart from Tiger calling him 'a clown' he didn't get in trouble.

At the 2022 Women's Open, American golfer Sophia Schubert tossed the ball to her caddie, Dean Robertson. He thought she wanted the ball discarded, so threw it over a stone wall into stinging nettles. But Sophia wanted the ball cleaned! Panic ensued, because if her ball couldn't be found, Sophia would receive penalty strokes added to her score. The caddie clambered over the wall and waded through the stinging nettles and found her ball just in time. Phew!

Top golfers don't necessarily make top caddies. That was the lesson Gary Nicklaus learned when he got his dad – the great Jack Nicklaus – to caddie for him. Whilst playing a qualifying round for the 1983 US Open, Jack realised that he had left one of his own clubs in his son's bag. The mistake cost Gary four shots and he failed to qualify. The Nicklaus family dinner that night must have been awkward!

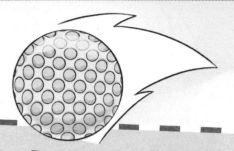

Eye of the Tiger

Name: Tiger Woods

Born: 1975

Country: USA

Professional tournament wins: 110

Major wins: 15

Super stat: Tiger has not one but 20 holes-in-one!

Famous for: Being one of the greatest golfers of all time, dominating the highly competitive PGA Tour for many years

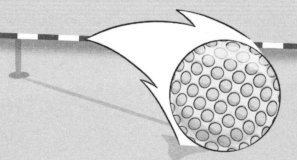

For almost 30 years the most famous golfer on the planet has been Eldrick Tont Woods, better known by the nickname given to him by his father: Tiger. Tiger was an incredible golfing prodigy. Aged two, he appeared on a TV show putting in front of the cameras. The following year he managed to play nine holes of a par-three golf course in less than 50 shots – incredible.

That was just the start! Tiger became obsessed with golf and improving his game. He was only five when he completed a full, 18-hole golf course in less than 100 shots, and eight when he managed to break 80. The same year, he won the first of six Junior World Championships. Tiger was going places!

"Talent is something you are born with, and a skill is something you develop. Ninety-nine percent of what you need to succeed in golf are skills."
– Tiger Woods

Tiger won three US Amateur Championships and went to Stanford University, but left to become a professional golfer in 1996. Some grizzled old golf fans wondered if this young man could compete with the battle-hardened players of the PGA Tour. A few even thought he might fail.

They were very, very wrong!

Tiger won two PGA events in 1996. The following year he secured his first major – the Masters by an incredible margin of 12 shots. He was only 21. The years that followed were definitely Tiger Time! Here's a flavour . . .

- *At the 2000 Open Championship, Tiger finished at 19 under par, an Open record. At the US Open the same year, he won by a huge margin: 15 shots ahead of second placed Ernie Els.*

- By the age of 25, he had won each of the four majors at least once, making him the youngest player to gain a Career Grand Slam. In total, he has won 15 majors and 82 PGA tournaments. He also nabbed 41 titles on the European Tour.

- He played 142 PGA tournaments in a row, making the cut to play in the last two rounds. He never failed to make a cut between 1998 and 2005.

- He spent an incredible 683 weeks as the world number one ranked player, more than double the record of the next best golfer.

DID YOU KNOW?

At a 2002 tournament in Hawaii, Tiger smashed a PGA-record breaking drive of 455m. Incredible!

The 2010s were troubling times for Tiger as injuries and other issues took their toll. He only played one tournament between August 2015 and the start of 2018 while he recovered from four operations on his back. He was ranked below the top 1000 golfers. People wondered if they would ever see him play again.

They needn't have worried. Tiger roared back, winning the 2018 PGA Tour Championship. The following year he entered the last round of the Masters just two shots off the lead. Tiger relished the pressure and played a great round to win his 15th major, more than ten years since his last. **Amazing!**

RED SHIRT SUNDAYS

Tiger gained a fearsome reputation as a 'closer'. This means if he was in the lead (or a share of the lead) entering the last round of a tournament, he never crumbled and, more often than not, won. Rivals quaked at the sight of him in his red shirt, which he always wore for the final round. He was relentless!

"I wear red on Sundays because my mom [Kultilda] thinks that's my power colour, and you know you should always listen to your mom."
— Tiger Woods

Are You Covered?

In Japan, hitting a hole-in-one also hits your wallet.
According to tradition, a player who makes a hole-
in-one should share their good luck with others. This
often takes the form of hosting a lavish party and
giving their guests gifts. Some of these parties can be
very expensive and so, from 1982, some Japanese
companies offered hole-
in-one insurance! These
policies pay out if a
genuine hole-in-one
occurs – enough to
hold a party and give
gifts. Around four million
golfers in Japan have this
insurance but only a few
ever get to make a claim.

Brilliance From Brittny

In 1991, Brittny Andreas scored a hole-in-one at the second hole of the Jimmy Clay Golf Course in Austin, Texas. What made it more extraordinary was that she was only six years old at the time!

Limited Edition

In 2008, Nike produced 2000 golf balls, each with their own serial number. The balls were coloured platinum and mixed randomly in golf ball sets. Twenty-four of these balls featured a picture of Tiger Woods swinging a golf club. Anyone who found one of these got the chance to play Tiger in a single-hole match!

Sandy Lie

Opened in 1976, the Coober Pedy Opal Fields golf course in Australia is different to most others... it has absolutely no grass. Although there are artificial grass tees to start each hole from, the rest of the course is sand, sand, sand. Players carry a small piece of artificial turf with them to place the ball on before they play their shot from the fairway. The greens are covered in oil, which is raked into the sand to make it stick together and not blow away. As a result, the course is mostly white with black-coloured greens.

Two in One

German golfer Kassandra Komma was playing the Sharf golf course in Michigan, USA, when she aced the 177-yard third hole. Wunderbar! Four holes later, she hit her second hole-in-one of the round on the par-three seventh. The chances of two holes-in-one in one round are estimated at a cool one-in-64 million!

DID YOU KNOW?

Only five male left-handed golfers so far have won majors: Bob Charles (from New Zealand), Mike Weir (Canada), Bubba Watson and Brian Harman (both USA) and the most famous leftie of them all, Phil Mickelson (USA), who has won six!

Gallant George

Canadian George Lyon made quite an impression at the 1904 Olympics. The 46 year old beat the other 74 competitors to win the golf event. He performed a somersault and then went up to receive his gold medal by walking on his hands! Four years later, George arrived in London to defend his Olympic title only to discover no one else had entered. A dispute between English and Scottish golfers meant they had all boycotted the event. The organising committee offered him the gold medal, but gallant George refused to accept it as he had not won it in competition.

Tree-mendous

During the first round of the 1979 US Open, cunning American Lon Hinkle chose a different route to get to the green of the eighth hole. Instead of driving the ball straight down the long eighth fairway, he took a big shortcut by aiming the ball through a gap in the trees to land his ball on the fairway of the neighbouring 17th hole. Tournament officials were not amused.

Overnight, the organisers bought a tree for US$120 and planted it to fill the gap that Lon had launched his ball through. Was Lon foiled? Nope. For his second/ next attempt, he just launched his shot higher, over the tree and onto the 17th. This left him a simple 6-iron shot to the next green!

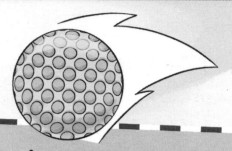

Losing Your Cool

Name: Brian Barnes

Born: 1945

Died: 2019

Country: England / UK

Professional tournament wins: 26

Major wins: 0

Super stat: Only player to beat Jack Nicklaus twice in the Ryder Cup…on the same day!

Famous for: Appearing in the Ryder Cup and being a leading player on the European Tour in its early days

Playing a good mental game is an important part of golf. Top players tend to be skilled at putting a bad shot to the back of their mind and focusing on making up for it with their next. However, even pro players sometimes lose their cool. Such was the case with English golfer Brian Barnes when he took part in the 1968 French Open. Brian played a great shot on the short par-three eighth hole on the Golf de Saint-Cloud course. He only needed a putt of just over a metre to make a birdie . . .

. . . but he pushed the putt wide. So he reached across the hole to tap the ball into the hole. Big mistake. You should always line up a putt properly, however short it is.

Brian missed.

Irritated and just wanting to get onto the next tee, he reached across the hole in a similar way to knock the ball in.

He missed again.

Doh!

Brian then struck the ball as it was moving. This incurred an extra-shot penalty from the marshals – because you're not allowed to strike a ball that is still rolling along the green.

Incensed, Brian carried on, putting the ball again and again without due care and attention and missing each time. The shots mounted up and when he straddled the ball and hit it between his legs, yet another penalty shot was added to his score.

By the time Brian finally stomped off the green in a major huff, he had registered 15 shots. So, he was 12 over par on a hole for which his first shot was less than 1.5m from the pin! Although it was curtains for Brian at that year's French Open, he did win the tournament seven years later. He won more than 20 tournaments in total and also played in six Ryder Cups, but he is always remembered for his meltdown in France on the eighth green.

DID YOU KNOW?

On the PGA Tour, the average maximum speed that the ball races away following a drive is 278.3km/h – faster than many sports cars.

Wrong Ball

Tournament golf has many extra rules that professionals must abide by. Poor Mark Hensby suffered from one of them during the 2021 Palmetto Championship in Congaree, South Carolina, USA. Mark had qualified for only two PGA Tour events in three years so was keen to do well. The Australian was on the eighth hole in his first round when he suddenly spotted that the ball he was playing wasn't his own. Gulp!

Mark had picked it up by mistake when putting on the practice greens before his round. This ball belonged to fellow pro golfer Pat Perez. Mark had taken the ball from his bag after losing one on the fourth hole and played on without realising it wasn't his.

Mark had to fess up, and two shots were added to his score for every hole he had used the illegal ball on – that's four holes, so eight shots. Poor Mark managed to shoot a very creditable 74 for his first round, but that became 84 with the penalty shots and he withdrew from the tournament distraught.

DID YOU KNOW?

In the 2019 Senior LPGA Championship, Lee Ann Walker wasn't aware that the rules didn't allow her caddie to help line up putts. Lee Ann was penalised two strokes for each time this happened and it happened 29 times, so she finished on 217 shots for just two rounds. Ouch!

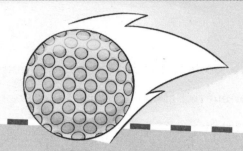

Rory McIlroy

Name: Rory McIlroy

Born: 1989

Country: Northern Ireland

Professional tournament wins: 37

Major wins: 4

Super stat: In 2019, Rory completed more than 500 weeks ranked within the world's top 10

Famous for: A former world number one golfer, four-time Ryder Cup winner and golfing superstar

When Tiger Woods suggests your new golfing nickname should be The Intimidator, you better be good. Fortunately for Rory Daniel McIlroy, he's one of the best.

As a child, Rory began playing with a set of plastic toy clubs at his home in Northern Ireland. He quickly started swinging so hard that the clubs shattered. Dad, Gerry, cut down a real golf club for him to use instead. Such was young Rory's talent, the committee at his local course, Holywood Golf Club, changed their rules to let him join the juniors even though he was only seven years old. By the time he was nine years old, Rory was winning the Under-10s World Championship in Miami, USA and appearing on TV, chipping balls into an open washing machine!

> **"From about the age of five, I told anyone who would listen that I was going to be the best golfer in the world."**
>
> – Rory McIlroy

By 16 years of age, Rory was hot property. He was courted by major US colleges offering him sports scholarships, but he decided to continue learning his golf in Europe. He set a new course record at Ireland's Royal Portrush Golf Club in 2005, won the European Amateur Championship in 2006 and, in 2007, turned professional at the age of 18. He raced up the world rankings, ending 2009 rated as the ninth best golfer in the world. Three years later, after winning the 2011 US Open and 2012 PGA Championship, he reached the pinnacle – he was the number one golfer in the world.

> **"Your success only makes you more motivated to do better."**
>
> – Rory McIlroy

At 1.75m, Rory is not as tall as some of his rivals, but he hits the ball a long way: in 2022, he averaged around 320 yards (293m). At the 2014 Scottish Open, Rory ripped a 436 yard (399m) drive straight-onto the green on a par four hole – that's a distance of four football pitches end to end!

Rory's phenomenal skill has seen him win more than 40 tournaments, including four majors. He's also appeared in seven Ryder Cups. The hunt for a fifth major still spurs him on and, in 2022, he got desperately close, eventually finishing runner-up to Scottie Scheffler at the Masters.

The following year, he finished runner-up at another major, the US Open, just one shot behind the winner, Wyndham Clark. In total, he has spent more than 120 weeks as world number one, more than any other European golfer.

DID YOU KNOW?

In 2014, Rory was playing the second round of the Tour Championship when he hit a wayward shot that bounced off a tree and straight into a spectator's trouser pocket! Rory was given a free drop for his ball and went on to record a five-under-par round of 65. Commenting afterwards, Rory said, "It's not the first time that's happened this year. I just had a ball go up someone's trouser leg at the Scottish Open in Aberdeen!"

Good Drive!

The Brickyard Crossing golf course is one with a difference. It's located beside and inside a world-famous racetrack, USA's Indianapolis Motor Speedway, home to the Indy 500 race. Golfers have to walk across the track to reach the seventh hole which, like the eighth, ninth and tenth, are located inside the oval racetrack. The golf course is obviously closed on race days!

Wrong Ball

The 15th hole at the Cape Kidnappers course in New Zealand is not for the faint-hearted. For starters, it is 650 yards (594m) long and the edge of the fairway and green end in cliffs with a 140m drop below!

Floating Green

The Coeur d'Alene golf course in Idaho, USA, has
something a little different . . . a green that floats.
The 14th hole is a par three, and its green is a floating
2,000-tonne island in the middle of a lake. Course
managers can operate underwater cables to move
the green and change the length of the hole.

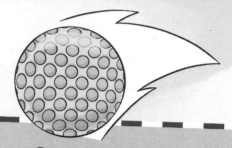

Dynamite Davies

Name: Laura Davies

Born: 1963

Country: England / UK

Professional tournament wins: 87

Major wins: 4

Super stat: She's the only player to have competed in 12 Solheim Cups

Famous for: A serial winner, dominant European player and the first Brit to top the LPGA Tour money list

Laura Davies is a 24-carat British golf legend and a member of the World Golf's Hall of Fame.

Laura first picked up a golf club at the age of ten, playing casual rounds at a public course with her dad and older brother Tony. Finding that she had to hit the ball really hard to keep up with her brother, the natural competitor in Laura came to the fore.

Laura loved sports. She played netball, football, field hockey and cricket, but by age 14, it was golf that captured her attention. During summer holidays, Laura and Tony would be dropped off at the golf course in the morning and play all day until their mother picked them up on the way back from work. By the time she was 16, Laura was a fine amateur golfer and could easily beat her brother!

Laura turned professional in 1985 and won her first pro tournament, the Belgian Ladies Open, the same year. She would eventually record a staggering 87 tournament wins. There may be more to come as Laura still plays between working as a TV golf commentator.

Laura had many amazing years in the sport. In fact, between 1985 and 2010, there was only one year (2005) in which she didn't win a professional tournament. One of her high points came in 1994 when she became the first golfer, male or female, to win events on five different golf tours around the world in a single calendar year.

Laura struck gold all over the world. She recorded three wins on the LPGA Tour in the USA, two on the Ladies European Tour, as well as victories on the

LPGA of Japan Tour, the ALPG in Australia, and the Ladies Asian Golf Tour during which she won the Thailand Open. In North America she finished top of the LPGA Tour money list – the first time a non-American had achieved that feat.

In 2004, Laura created two new records. She made the most eagles (19!) on the LPGA Tour and, when she entered the ANZ Championship, she also became the first woman to compete in a men's European Tour event.

"I just love competing, love mixing with the youngsters and spending time with them. My whole life has been competitive sport and I don't want to turn my back on it yet."

– Laura Davies

In 2018, the LPGA launched the first US Senior Women's Open tournament for top players over the age of 50. Laura was 55 when she won the tournament by an incredible ten shots. Her four rounds of 71, 71, 66 and 68 put her at −16. Second place went to US legend Juli Inkster on −6. The same year, she won the other major senior women's tournament, the Women's Senior LPGA Championship, this time four shots clear of her rivals. Laura managed a 'senior slam' the very first time it was possible!

DID YOU KNOW?

Laura built a nine-hole golf course of sorts in her back garden. It featured one full-sized green and bunker, plus nine different tees to practise from!

Tin Cup

Tin Cup is a 1996 movie starring Kevin Costner. The main character is a talented golfer who cannot help but go for the most attacking shot every time, even when it would be wiser to play safe.

Playing safe was rarely what John Daly did. This American golfer earned his nickname 'Wild Thing' for taking risks and driving the ball longer and harder than his rivals. John was a bit of a maverick who sometimes got into trouble with golf officials. But he won plenty of fans and two majors – the PGA Championship in 1991 and the Open in 1995 – with displays of all-out attacking golf.

At the 1998 Bay Hill Invitational tournament, John made history with a crazy display of bravado in the final round at the 543-yard, par-five sixth hole. John was two under par for the tournament when he reached the tee. By the time he had finished the hole, he was 11 over! Let's break down precisely what happened . . .

Shots	What happened
1-2	Driver in the water, penalty stroke
3-4	3–wood in the water, penalty stroke
5-6	3–wood in the water, penalty stroke
7-8	3–wood in the water, penalty stroke
9-10	3–wood in the water, penalty stroke
11-12	3–wood in the water, penalty stroke
13-14	3–wood clears the water but lands in a hazard, penalty stroke
15	6–iron hits rocks near the green and the ball bounces into bunker
16	Sand wedge from bunker onto the green
17	First putt misses hole
18	Second putt – ball drops into the hole. Phew!

A major-winning pro golfer had taken 18 shots on a par-five hole!

Each time John struck the ball into the water, he casually stretched out his hand to his caddie and asked for another ball. He sincerely thought that the next time he played the shot, it would be different and he would clear the water.

> **"I had the courage to keep going for it, but I didn't have the wisdom to bail out right . . . I still say they made that movie [*Tin Cup*] about me!"**
>
> – John Daly

John strode off onto the next tee, where he promptly made a birdie! Not that it helped a great deal. He finished his round with a score of 85 and ended up 53rd at the tournament.

An Oldie But a Goldie

In 1907, Elsie McLean scored a hole-in-one at the fourth hole of the Bidwell Park golf course in California, USA. Not a big deal, you would think. Hundreds of golfers grabbed a hole-in-one every year. So why was Elsie suddenly invited to appear on US national TV shows? Well, it was because of her age – Elsie was 102 years old at the time and had been playing at the same golf course for 75 years!

"I said, 'Oh my Lord. It can't be true. It can't be true.' I was so excited. And the girls were absolutely overcome. For an old lady, I still hit the ball pretty good."

– Elsie McLean

Elsie played golf three times a week at the course but had never hit a hole-in-one before. She continued playing until she was 105 years old. Even then, she would come out and ride a golf cart alongside her golf-playing friends and sometimes hit a few balls. She remains the oldest golfer to hit a hole-in-one anywhere in the world.

DID YOU KNOW?

At the prestigious Open Championship in 1983, American Hale Irwin tried to tap in a 15cm-long putt backhanded . . . and missed. Oops! He was annoyed at the time but even more annoyed at the end when he lost the championship by just one shot. Ouch!

One-Club Challenge

In 1985, a World One-Club Championship was held. Players could pick any club from their golf bag with which to play an entire round. The competition was won by American' Thad Daber who used a 6-iron for each of his shots – including putts. Thad completed a full 18-hole round in just 73 strokes. Highly impressive.

Two years later at the Lochmere Golf Club in North Carolina, USA, he won again, this time shooting a two-under-par score of 70. Great stuff! In total, Thad has won the championship four times and has been a golf pro for more than 30 years.

Handy Work

How many golf balls can you hold in one hand?
If you dare to find out, make sure you do it standing
on grass – not pavement or concrete – so that any
dropped balls don't bounce away. Five, six or seven
is good. However, in 2012, Italian marvel Silvio
Sabba managed to hold 27! Silvio is a personal
trainer and a bit of a serial world record breaker. His
past exploits include most toilet rolls stacked with one
hand and most underpants put on in 30 seconds
(16 pairs)!

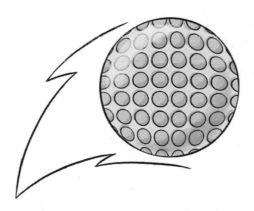

Looooong Holes

Tourists often visit the Japanese town of Sano to play a round at Satsuki Golf Club. The biggest draw is its monster seventh hole. It is a par seven and measures a whopping 964 yards (881m) long. Amazingly, Japan is no longer home to the longest hole. That's now found in South Korea at the Gunsan Country Club. Its third hole stretches an incredible 1,093 yards (1,003m) – that's two-and-a-half times round a full-sized running track!

DID YOU KNOW?

American Michelle Wie West was just ten years old when she qualified to play in the US Women's Amateur Public Links Championship against adults. She went on to win 29 amateur tournaments and turned professional before her 16th birthday.

Big Bunker

The world's deepest bunker is called Nunca Sera, which means 'will never be' in Portuguese. It's found on the 13th hole of the Pura Ficção golf course in Portugal. If your ball is plugged in the bottom part of the bunker, you have to hit a shot at least 22m into the air to clear its top lip.

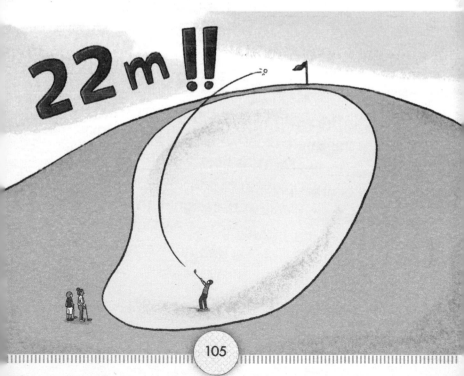

Oldest Game

Whilst we think of golf as originating in Scotland, it's possible it might actually have come from China. Around 1,000 years ago during the Song Dynasty (960–1279 CE), the game of chuiwan (meaning 'to hit ball') became popular. It involved people hitting a wooden ball into holes marked by coloured flags dug into the ground. Sound familiar?

DID YOU KNOW?

The world's biggest golf facility is in Shenzhen, China. Mission Hills contains an incredible **11** 18-hole championship golf courses plus an all-par-three course as well! Each course is designed by a different legend, including Jack Nicklaus, Greg Norman, Ernie Els and Annika Sörenstam.

Crazy Golf

This fun putting game is known by many names, including minigolf, putt-putt and adventure golf. The first crazy-golf course in the USA opened in 1916 and was called Thistle Dhu. By the 1930s, there were 150 courses in New York City alone, mostly located on the flat roofs of tall buildings.

Today, crazy-golf courses are found everywhere from shopping centres, theme parks and the decks of cruise ships. Some have themes, such as Dino Park in Thailand, which includes models of a T. rex and an erupting volcano to putt round. Others are just bonkers, like Par King in Illinois, USA, which includes clowns, armoured knights and a three-metre-tall rollercoaster for your ball to take a ride on.

Top Bob

In 2007, Sir Bob Charles recorded a second round of 68 at the New Zealand Open to become the oldest golfer to make the cut at a European Tour event. He was 71 years old. He retired in 2010 with a record of 80 tournament wins – including the Open Championship all the way back in 1963!

One to Forget

In 1990, American Patty Sheehan won five times on the LPGA Tour, but the US Women's Open is one event she would love to forget. During the third round, she'd built up a huge 12-shot lead over her rivals. But in the fourth round, it all went wrong. Patty recorded bogey after bogey to lose the tournament by a single stroke. Ouch!

Repeat Success

John Hudson was a 25-year-old English professional golfer struggling at the 1971 Martini International tournament when he did something absolutely extraordinary. John aced the 195-yard 11th hole with his drive landing two metres from the pin then rolling in. A hole-in-one! **Amazing!** He then stepped up onto the tee of the 311-yard, par-four 12th hole, and did the same again. John was five under for the two holes and it's the only known time in professional golf that a player has made consecutive holes-in-one. He finished the tournament in ninth place and received £160 in prize money.

Golf in a Jetstream

In 1952, the Royal Thai Air Force built the Kantarat Golf Course in Thailand. The 18-hole course is located between the runways of Bangkok's Don Muang Airport. You have to pass through airport security before you can play a round. Once on the course, you get to see airliners taking off and landing from extremely close up. Hope the noise of their jet engines doesn't put you off your game!

DID YOU KNOW?

The Akureyri Golf Club in Iceland is thought to be the most northerly permanent golf course in the world. Every June, a time of year when the Sun doesn't set there, the club holds the Arctic Open. Competitors have to be night owls because some tee-off times are 10 p.m., and play can continue until 3 a.m.

Coast-to-Coast

Professional golf teacher Floyd Rood headed inland from the Pacific coast of the USA in September 1963. His aim was to play the entire width of the country as a single golf course, west to east, finishing with a shot into the Atlantic Ocean. It took Rood 13 months and 114,737 shots to complete the feat. It is reported that he lost over 3,500 balls along the way!

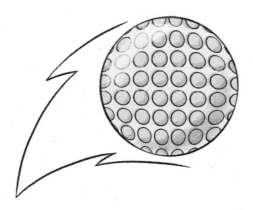

Time For Tee

In 1899, an African–American dentist called Dr George Grant invented the first wooden golf tee. Until that time, golfers raised their ball up on the teeing area for a drive by moulding a small pillar out of sand and water – messy work. George didn't make money from his invention; instead, he handed out tees for free to family and friends.

Twenty-two years later, another American dentist called William Lowell launched the Reddy Tee. He carved the prototype out of a piece of flagpole using his dentistry tools! The Reddy Tee was made of birch wood and painted bright red to make it easily visible in green grass.

Sales were slow until William had a brainwave.

He paid popular pro golfer Walter Hagen US$1,500 to endorse his tees and use them in tournaments and exhibitions. Spectators began scrambling for tees left on the course after Hagen drove his ball. Sales were brisk and soon other companies were making tees as well.

Record Setter

The last amateur golfer to win a PGA tournament was Phil Mickelson in 1991. Phil turned professional the following year and has won a further 44 PGA Tour events. These include the 2021 PGA Championship at the age of 50 years and 11 months – making Phil the oldest major winner ever.

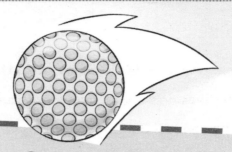

Super-Quick Collin

Name: Collin Morikawa

Born: 1997

Country: USA

Professional tournament wins: 6

Major wins: 2

Super stat: From his PGA debut, made 22 cuts at tournaments in a row, second only to Tiger Woods

Famous for: His meteoric rise as a golf pro and, in 2021, becoming the first American to finish the year as the European Tour's number one player

Some pro golfers can spend years on the LPGA, European or other tours, before winning a tournament. Collin Morikawa waited only seven weeks. He turned pro in June 2019 and the following month won the Barracuda Open, pocketing a whopping prize of US$630,000. Wow! It was only his sixth PGA tour event.

The following year was his first full PGA season. Collin played in the prestigious PGA Championship for the first time. After three rounds, he was in a good position: one of twelve players within three shots of the lead. After a further nine holes, Collin was joint leader with six other players, all on ten under par. It was a gripping contest.

He was the first to make a move, making a birdie to go 11 under at the 14th hole. He then applied the killer blow on the 16th. Ripping his driver off the tee, Collin's shot landed on the green just two metres away from the hole. He sank the putt to make an eagle and go two shots clear of all his opponents.

Under great pressure from his competitors, Collin needed to hold his nerve on the last two holes. He managed to keep his cool, becoming a major winner at just 23 years of age. With the trophy came a whopping winner's prize – a cool US$1.98 million.

There's more! The following year, he crossed the Atlantic Ocean to play in the Open Championship for the first time. The tournament was held at the Royal St George's Golf Club in Kent, but Collin wasn't put off by the course's tough reputation.

"I came out this week not worried about playing against everyone else. I'm just trying to learn the golf course."

– Collin at the 2021 Open

In fact, he shot a record low score of 265 for his four rounds and scooped another big payday of US$2.07 million. The victory made him the only golfer in history to win two majors on the first attempts. **Cool.**

In the Bag

For centuries, you could play with as many golf clubs as you (or your caddie) could carry. A famous American golfer called Lawson Little Junior won a number of amateur and professional tournaments with 26 clubs in his bag, including seven or eight different designs of wedge. It is said that he even played some competitions with 31 clubs. Crazy!

In 1938, golf authorities added a new rule, that made sore-backed caddies rejoice. The maximum number of clubs in a golfer's bag was set at 14. Any more and either strokes would be added to your score or you would be thrown out of the tournament. Even with the new rule in place, Lawson went on to arguably his greatest triumph, winning the 1940 US Open Championship by beating American pro Gene Sarazen in a play-off.

Even though the rule has been in force for over 80 years, even professional players sometimes fall foul of it. At the 2022 Houston Open, PGA pro golfer Mark Hubbard was disqualified during his second round when he added a 15th club to his bag.

Plop!

The 17th hole at the TPC course at Sawgrass Stadium in the USA is only 137 yards (125m) long. But this par three terrifies many golfers because its green is set in a deep lake. Apart from a narrow pathway, the small green is completely surrounded by water. Golfers have to pitch the ball high and get their distance and line perfect, otherwise their ball will land in the water.

Judging by the estimated 100,000 balls lost in the lake each year, many golfers get their aim wrong! At the 1998 Players Championship, Brad Fabel seemed to avoid trouble when his ball landed safely on the green. His thoughts turned to the possibility of a birdie . . . but not the one that waddled onto the green . . .

A seagull loomed over his ball and picked it up. The bird struggled to keep Brad's ball in its beak as it flew away and ended up dropping it in the water. Fortunately, the rules allowed Brad to place a fresh ball on the same spot on the green without any penalty strokes. Unfortunately, after all that commotion, he couldn't get a birdie . . . or a par. He three-putted for a bogey.

Un-dress Code

Many golf club have a strict dress code. La Jenny in La Porge, France, is a bit different. The six-hole course is part of a naturist resort and when the weather allows, golfers play a round in the nude!

DID YOU KNOW?

A new type of golf ball was launched by the B. F. Goodrich Company in 1905. Their pneumatic golf balls had cores filled with compressed air. The balls flew a long way, but in hot weather the air inside them heated up and caused some balls to explode!

Go Ko!

In 2009, Lydia Ko won a major amateur tournament in New Zealand. It was the North Island Women's Under-19 Championship and Lydia was just 11 years old! Just three years later, Lydia became the youngest girl or boy to win a professional golf tour event when she won the Women's NSW Open in Australia. Amazingly, she'd nearly won the NSW Open the year before at age 13, but missed an easy putt on the last green.

DID YOU KNOW?

Measuring 3,908m², the ninth green at the USA's Springlake Golf and Tennis Resort's Osprey Course is the world's largest – about the size of eight basketball courts!

Footgolf

A variant of golf replaces golf balls with full-sized footballs, and golf clubs with a player's feet! Footgolf was pioneered in the Netherlands almost 20 years ago, although similar sports such as Buschball in Germany began earlier. Footgolf courses have sprung up in the UK and other European countries and are often located on regular pitch-and-putt or par-three golf courses. The main difference is a far bigger hole (50–52cm in diameter) for players to 'putt' the football into.

The sport even has its own global championship, the FIFG Footgolf World Cup, which was first held in Hungary in 2012. In 2023, the World Cup came to Orlando, Florida. Some 972 players took part, with France crowned the men's world champions, and Japan the women's world champions.

Hot Streak

In 1948, Byron Nelson had the hottest winning streak in PGA golf history. He won an incredible 18 tournaments, including eleven in a row. Brilliant Byron was untouchable, but also unlucky that only one major, the PGA Championship, was played that year (which of course he won).

DID YOU KNOW?

Golfers at the Jinga Golf Club in Uganda are allowed a free drop of their ball if it lands in a hippopotamus footprint. They must also stop playing and give way to the elephants that occasionally roam the course!

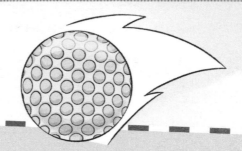

Body No Barrier

Name: Jennifer Sräga

Born: 2000

Country: Germany

Professional tournament wins: 0

Major wins: 0

Super stat: Jennifer's handicap of three puts her in the top one per cent of women golfers

Famous for: Raising awareness of golf for those with disabilities and inspiring others to take up the sport

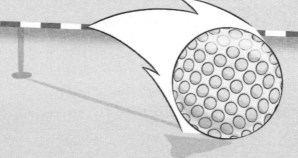

German Jennifer Sräga was born with a genetic condition called achondroplasia, which means she has shorter limbs than most people. As a child, Jennie got into golf and, along with her older sister Steffi, found she loved the challenge of playing.

> **"When I started thinking properly and practising, I realised that I could beat others. I had to learn to believe in myself."**
> – Jennifer Sräga

Jennie, with a shorter swing than other golfers, couldn't gain as much distance. However, she learned to compensate for this with superb touch and flair close to the green, and she worked hard to make her putting as accurate as possible. Within a few years, she was taking part in tournaments, and got her handicap down to three – an impressive feat.

In 2022, Jennie was selected to play in a special short tournament held before the Open Championship at St Andrews in Scotland. She played alongside legends of the game including Tiger Woods, Henrik Stenson and Gary Player, held before the Open Championship at St Andrews.

DID YOU KNOW?

No one, not even Tiger Woods, has won more major tournaments than Jack Nicklaus. The 'Golden Bear' triumphed at 18 majors, including six Masters. That's not all. In total, he won an incredible 118 professional tournaments and made an amazing 21 holes-in-one in competition. Awesome.

Achoo!

Imagine being a professional golfer who suffers from a grass allergy! That's what Steve Elkington discovered when he visited doctors in 1994 after suffering a terrible slump in his play. The doctors prescribed medicine and soon Steve was back in action and performing well. The following year, he won his first major, the PGA Championship.

Tree-iron

At the 1982 Fulford International tournament, German pro Bernhard Langer's ball at the 17th hole was found resting on a tree branch five metres above the ground. Instead of taking the penalty shot, Langer climbed up the tree, kept his balance and hit a remarkable shot onto the green.

12 vs 12

Every couple of years or so, a dozen of the best male or female golfers from Europe battle 12 from the USA in drama-fuelled contests. These head-to-head cup competitions (the Ryder Cup for men and the Solheim Cup for women) attract huge crowds and TV audiences. The Ryder Cup began in 1927 when it used to be Great Britain vs USA. After a number of thrashings in a row and an overall scoreline of 22–3 to the USA, the Brits turned to Europe for help. And how well did they do? Incredibly well! In the 21st Century, Europe has won seven and lost just three of the ten Ryder Cups played so far.

The Solheim Cup began in 1990. Like the Ryder Cup, it sees pairs of players from each team battle it out until, in the last round, each player is pitted against just one opponent. At stake in each match is a winning point (or a half point for both players if the match is 'halved', meaning drawn). All the points go towards the teams' overall tallies.

With 28 matches played, 14 ½ points is enough to win the Cup, a score Europe's men managed in both 2010 and 2012, and Europe's women in 2015 and 2019. Phew! That's how tight many of these cup competitions can be.

TOP POINT SCORERS

In the Ryder Cup, no one has topped the Spanish pairing of Seve Ballesteros and José María Olazábel. They played together as a pair in 15 matches, winning 11 and halving two. In the Solheim Cup, it is the mighty Laura Davies from England (see p92-96) with the biggest points total of 25 wins and six halves.

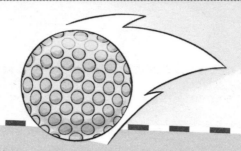

Winning Ways

Name: Kipp Popert

Born: 1998

Country: England / UK

Professional tournament wins: 6

Major wins: 0

Super stat: Kipp won the 2022 Australian All-Abilities Championship by a record seven shots

Famous for: Being ranked the world's number one golfer with a disability

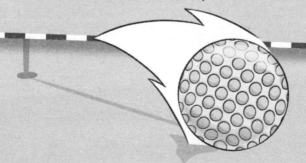

In 2022, English player Kipp Popert managed to qualify for the Amateur Championship held at Royal Lytham and St Annes in northwest England. He was the first golfer with a disability to do so.

Kipp was born with a condition called cerebral palsy, which greatly affected the growth and movement of his legs and feet. He has had ten operations, including major reconstructions of both feet. These were frustrating times – there were long stays in hospital and he had to re-learn how to walk and play golf.

> **"If I was playing somebody more able-bodied than me, I saw that as an awesome opportunity to beat them and get better."**
>
> – Kipp Popert

Kipp mostly competed in local and regional tournaments with able-bodied golfers – until he was watching an EDGA tournament for disabled golfers on TV in 2019. He played his first EDGA event the same year and, in 2022, won five tournaments on the newly-formed G4D (Golf for the Disabled) Tour, making him the G4D world number one.

Animal Antics

Players at South Africa's Skukuza Golf Club have
to contend with plenty of truly WILD wildlife. Not
surprising, as the course is situated inside the Kruger
National Park wildlife sanctuary. It's not unusual to
find hyenas on the fairways, baboons on the green
and warthogs in the rough! Occasionally, a herd of
elephants will wander onto the course, which causes
havoc on the carefully prepared soft greens!

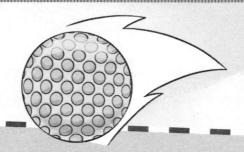

Inspiring Others

Name: Pak Se-ri

Born: 1977

Country: South Korea

Professional tournament wins: 39

Major wins: 5

Super stat: Won the longest tournament in women's golf – the 1998 US Women's Open – which ran to 20 play-off holes after the regular 72 holes were completed

Famous for: Hall of Fame player who inspired a new generation of South Korean female golfers

In 1998, a Korean golf sensation announced herself to the world. Pak Se-ri was in her first season on the full LPGA tour in the USA and won not only the Women's PGA Championship, but also the Women's US Open the same year. At just 20, she was the youngest women's US Open winner at the time.

Millions cheered her every shot back in South Korea, including nine-year-old Inbee Park and her parents, who were huge golf fans. Se-ri was the only South Korean on the tour at the time, but she inspired an explosion in Korean women's golf. Thousands of young girls, known as the Se-ri Kids, took up the game and Inbee was amongst them. She proved a natural and became part of a wave of talented Koreans who really impacted women's golf.

In 2007, Inbee joined the LPGA tour in the USA, and the following year triumphed at the US Open. She finished her four rounds at the Interlachen Country Club at nine under par, four shots ahead of second place Helen Alfredsson. Two of her countrywomen, In-Kyung Kim and Mi Hyun Kim, also finished in the top ten. At 19 years of age, Inbee had broken Pak Se-ri's record as the youngest US Open winner.

> **"If I could do what Pak did, that will be very, very good. Maybe in later years I can really teach all these little kids to reach their dreams."**
>
> – Inbee Park

After this stellar start came a dip in form, and Inbee struggled to gain another win on tour. Her game was still evolving, especially her extremely accurate putting. She made a decision to not rip at the ball on drives and long shots, and instead sacrificed a little distance in exchange for greater accuracy. When it all came together, she started to dominate.

Her next important tournament win was the Evian Masters in 2012. That year saw her play with remarkable consistency. She finished in the top three in ten of the 23 tournaments she played. The following year, Inbee won six times on the tour,

including scooping three of the four majors.
She ended the year as the world's number one
ranked female golfer.

> ## "I realised I had won the gold for the whole country, not just for myself."
> – Inbee Park

In 2016, golf returned to the Olympic Games for the first time since 1904. Inbee was there and won the tournament by five strokes. She added a gold medal to her seven major victories and 21 tour wins overall.

Just like Pak before her, Inbee's exploits were watched on late night television back in South Korea and helped inspire a new generation of up-and-coming Korean golfers. In June 2023, 14 of the top 50 ranked women golfers in the world were South Korean.

One-Handed Hole-in-one

Canadian Laurent Hurtubise was born with a right arm that ends just below the elbow. Determined not to be held back, Laurent threw himself into sports, playing baseball and taking up golf when he was 11 – playing solely with his left arm.

Fifty years later, he got the chance to take part in a PGA Pro-Am (where professional golfers play rounds with amateur players) in California, USA. Whilst playing with PGA pros Greg Chalmers and Troy Merritt, Laurent hit a great 6-iron on the par-three fourth hole. The ball sailed away, landed on the front of the green and, to everyone's amazement, rolled straight into the hole!

Astonishingly, it was Laurent's third hole-in-one during his career, but the only one that was televised. Clips of his feat went viral.

**"That was the coolest experience
I've had on the golf course…
He's an inspiration."**
– PGA pro Troy Merritt on Laurent's hole-in-one

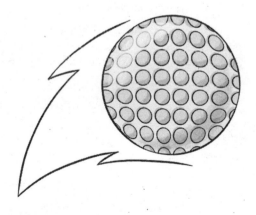

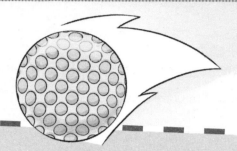

Moon Golf

Name: Alan Shepard

Born: 1923

Died: 1998

Country: USA

Professional tournament wins: 0

Major wins: 0

Super stat: Alan spent a total of nine days and 57 minutes in space on two space flights

Famous for: Being the first, and so far, only player to attempt a golf shot on the Moon

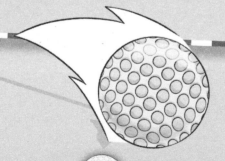

In 1961, Alan Shepard became the first US astronaut to head into space. Ten years later, he was part of the Apollo 14 mission that landed on the Moon.

Alan was also a keen amateur golfer and wanted to do something special on the Moon during his Apollo mission. So he asked a club maker in Texas to create a modified club head, a 6-iron, which he sneaked into his spacesuit before launch. Alan hid his golf balls inside a sock!

Along with fellow astronaut Edgar Mitchell, Alan spent over nine hours outside their spacecraft on the Moon's surface, performing all sorts of experiments and tasks. Alan saw his chance as they were heading back to their Lunar Module, and dropped a golf ball onto the Moon's surface. Then he whipped out his special club – the 6-iron head fitted to the handle of a spacecraft tool.

> **"Unfortunately, the suit is so stiff, I can't do this with two hands, but I'm going to try a little sand-trap shot here."**
>
> – Alan Shepard

With the Moon's gravity being less than one-sixth of Earth's, it was expected that a good shot would sail a long distance. However, Alan's bulky spacesuit meant he had to swing one-handed. He scuffed his first shot, which flew off into a small lunar crater.

Alan connected better with his second and told Mission Control that the ball had sailed 'miles and miles'. However, he wouldn't be the first or last golfer to exaggerate! We now think that the ball only travelled 35–40m, but it remains the longest shot played on the Moon. The balls are still there, but the club came back to Earth and is now kept in the USGA Golf Museum.

Disc Golf

Leave your clubs and balls at home because this version of the sport is played with Frisbees! Well, the discs used are a little smaller than your usual flying disc thrown at the beach. They also come in different designs for different shots just like clubs in regular golf. There are disc golf drivers, mid range discs (like 5-, 6- and 7-irons in regular golf) and putters.

Just like regular golf courses, players play rounds, but with shorter holes because discs don't fly as far as golf balls. Holes include obstacles such as hills, trees and water hazards. Players have to aim their disc to fly into a metal basket lined with chains – a good shot makes a distinctive CLANG as the disc hits the chains and lands in the basket.

From small beginnings in the 1970s, disc golf has boomed. There are more than 12,000 courses around the world, as well as professional players and international tournaments with tens of thousands of pounds of prize money.

19th Hole

You've finished our whirlwind round of golf's most amazing courses, players and moments, but our book hasn't finished yet!

Turn the page to find a simple player's guide, a glossary, plus a quiz to test your golfing knowledge . . .

How to Play: Basics

A round of golf is usually played over 18 holes. If playing a nine-hole course, golfers play twice to make a round.

Each hole begins in a marked-out teeing area (also known as a tee box). Players take their drive (their first shot on the hole) from here. Each hole ends with a closely-mown, smooth grass area called the green. Sunk within the green is a 10.8cm-wide hole marked by a flagpole called the pin. That's what you're aiming for.

In between tee and green can be all sorts of hazards to avoid, from trees and tall grass to hollows filled with sand (called bunkers), and entire streams, rivers and lakes. Every golf hole is different, which makes up part of the challenge.

Many golf holes have a corridor of mown grass between the tee and the green. This is called the fairway. It's usually a good idea to land your ball on there if you can!

Players strike the ball with a swing of their golf club. They vary how long their swing is depending on how far they want the ball to go. They can also control the distance and flight path of their shot by choosing the right golf club.

Club Talk

Players carry a putter, which is used to putt the ball smoothly across the green. They also carry a collection of up to 13 other clubs known as 'woods' and irons. Woods were once made of wood, but are now made of metals like stainless steel or titanium. A 1-wood is called a 'driver' and is the longest club in a golfer's bag. It sends the ball low but far – providing it's swung well.

The larger the number on an iron or wood, the greater the 'loft' (the angle the club face is tilted back from the vertical). A more lofted club sends the ball higher into the air. The most lofted clubs are called 'wedges', and these are used for short-distance shots and getting out of hazards, such as bunkers.

Scoring

Each shot played or attempted by the golfer is added to their score on a hole. If you play an air shot – swinging the club but missing the ball – tough luck, that's still a shot. You mark your score after each hole on a scorecard and add them up to gain your score for the round. In strokeplay competitions such as the US Women's Open or the PGA Championship, the

winner is the player who completes four rounds of
golf in the least number of shots.

DID YOU KNOW?

For a stunt in 1991, John Daly drove a ball
down a rock-solid runway at Denver Airport
in the USA. The ball sailed through the air
some 360 yards and then bounced along the
runway a further 450 yards, making it an
810-yard (740m) drive!

Rules, rules, rules

Golf has A LOT of rules. One of the most important is
playing the ball as it lies. The 'lie' is where a golf ball
comes to rest. Sometimes, it will not be a good lie –
if it lands in a tuft of grass or moss, for example. Bad
luck! You must play the ball without moving it
to a better lie.

If you hit the ball into a place where you cannot play a shot, such as up against the trunk of a tree, you have an unplayable lie. You add a penalty shot to your score and can move the ball up to two club lengths away, but not nearer the hole.

The edge of a course is marked by 'out of bounds' poles and signs. If you hit your ball out of bounds, you need to add one penalty shot to your score and play another ball from the same place. So, if you hit your drive (first shot on a hole) out of bounds, you drive again, but this is now your third shot on the hole.

Etiquette

In addition to the rules of the sport, golf expects players to behave well on the course. This includes things like replacing divots (the chunks of turf that can be dug up by some shots), and being quiet and still when someone else is about to play their shot.

Here are a few more examples of proper etiquette on the golf course:

- Don't dawdle. Play your shot and then walk briskly to your ball for your next shot so that golfers behind aren't kept waiting.

- Phones off! A distracting beep or ring tone as someone else plays a shot is unfair.

- Use the rake to remove your footprints from the sand bunker.

- Always shout '**Fore!**' if your shot veers off line and is heading towards other golfers or spectators.

Match the Fact

Can you match the golfer to their fact?

Answers on p159.

1. This player became the first LPGA player to finish the season averaging less than 70 shots for every round of golf she played. She won an amazing 72 LPGA tournaments and was made player of the year a record eight times.

2. This South African golfer always played in black and won an incredible 163 tournaments, travelling over 22 million kilometres in the process. The last of his nine majors came in 1978.

3. This English player has the unusual record of being the youngest player at three different Solheim Cups, being only 17 when selected for the European team in 2013. At 12, she left school and was taught at home, so that she could concentrate more on her golf.

4. This legendary Spanish golfer won five majors, playing shots no other golfers dared to attempt, and was a huge crowd favourite. He formed an incredible partnership in the Ryder Cup with José María Olazábal; the pair played 15 matches, winning 11 and drawing two.

5. The daughter of a grand-slam-winning tennis player, she won the PGA Championship in 2021 to become the number one golfer in the world rankings. The year before, she won a gold medal at the Olympic Games.

6. This golfer has shown exceptional dominance, winning two PGA tournaments eight times each and another pair of PGA tournaments seven times each. He is the only player to have won the US Junior, US Amateur and US Open, not once but three times each!

7. This New Zealand golfer won a record ten events on the LPGA tour before she was 19 years old.

These included the 2012 CN Canadian Women's Open when she was just 15.

8. 'Supermex' wowed fans and rival golfers alike with his jokes (he once threw a rubber snake at Jack Nicklaus whilst on a green), but he was a deadly serious golfer too. He won 92 tournaments including six majors. Extra impressive, because he had the likes of Tom Watson and Jack Nicklaus to battle against.

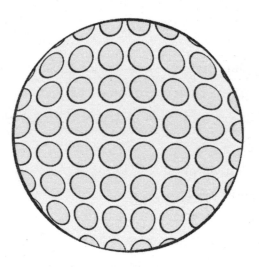

Match The Fact Answers

1. Annika Sörenstam
2. Gary Player
3. Charley Hull
4. Severiano Ballesteros
5. Nelly Korda
6. Tiger Woods
7. Lydia Ko
8. Lee Trevino

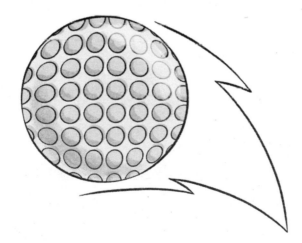

Glossary

ALBATROSS Completing a hole in three shots under par, usually by holing your second shot on a par-five or having a hole-in-one on a par-four hole.

BIRDIE Finishing a hole one shot under par.

BOGEY Completing a hole one shot over par.

BUNKER A depression on the course filled with sand, which must be raked after a shot is taken. Also known as a sand trap.

CADDIE A person who carries a player's bag of clubs and may advise them about what club and shot to play.

DOGLEG A golf hole with a sharp bend in its fairway. Often, players cannot see the green from the tee on a dogleg.

DRIVE The first shot on a hole made from the teeing area.

DROP When a golfer's ball is in a place from where they cannot play their next shot. The ball is dropped nearby but not closer to the hole.

EAGLE Completing a hole in two shots less than par.

FAIRWAY The corridor of cut grass between the tee and the green found on most golf holes.

FREE DROP When a player's ball is dropped and no penalty strokes are added to their score.

FORE! A warning shouted by golfers when they miss-hit a shot and fear the ball may be heading towards other people.

GRAND SLAM To win all the different major tournaments.

HANDICAP A system used in amateur golf to give players of different abilities a chance to play against each other on an equal footing.

HAZARD Features of a golf course, such as bunkers, ditches, streams or lakes, that make the course more challenging.

LOFT The angle of the club face, which affects the loft of the ball when struck.

LPGA Short for the Ladies Professional Golf Association. This body runs women's golf in the USA as well as organising tournaments elsewhere.

MAJOR The four most highly-prized tournaments in men's golf – the Masters, Open Championship, PGA Championship and US Open. In women's golf, there are currently five majors: The Chevron Championship, US Women's Open, Women's PGA Championship, the

Evian Championship and the Women's Open.

PAR The number (usually three, four or five, but sometimes six or seven) of shots a golf course feels that a hole should be completed in by a skilled player.

PGA Short for Professional Golf Association, this organisation runs golf in the USA. Its PGA tour is the largest tour, attracting top professional golfers from all over the world.

PROFESSIONAL To be paid to play golf either through appearance fees, winning prize money at tournaments or being sponsored by companies.

PUTT A shot made on the green (or close to it) in which the ball is rolled along the ground using the putter.

ROUND The word used for playing all the holes that make up a golf course.

TEE The rectangular area at the start of a golf hole from where players make their first shot (their drive). It's also the small plastic or wooden peg used to raise the ball off the ground when players take their first shot on a hole.

YARDAGE The distance from the tee to the flag on a golf course. Top players or their caddies carry charts showing detailed distances to all the major points on a golf hole.

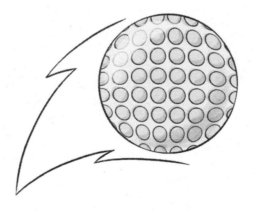

INCREDIBLE CRICKET

60 TRUE STORIES
EVERY FAN NEEDS TO KNOW

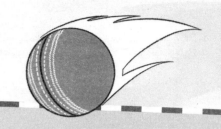

Oh, Jimmy, Jimmy!

Name: James Anderson

Born: Burnley, England, 1982

Nickname: Jimmy

Country: England / UK

Clubs: Auckland, Lancashire

Position: Bowler (right-arm, fast-medium)

Famous for: Outstandingly accurate swing bowling

Fast bowling is really hard work. You have to sprint in, leap and hurl your body forward, whirling your arm over as fast as possible to bowl the ball quickly and on target. Then you have to trudge all the way back to the top of your run-up and do it all over again. James Anderson, known to his fans as Jimmy, has done this more than 37,900 times for England in Test matches alone.

Then, there have been 9,584 balls bowled by Jimmy in ODIs and thousands and thousands more for his first club, Burnley, then his county side, Lancashire. In 2022, he turned 40 years old. When Jimmy first played for Burnley Cricket Club in 1998, his England teammate Ollie Pope was just four months old, while Sam Curran and Harry Brook hadn't even been born!

Jimmy made his England debut in ODIs in 2002 and in Tests the following year. He has played in Test matches every year since, 177 of them so far, taking 675 wickets – the most of any fast bowler.

What's more, he shows no signs of retiring. In fact, his bowling figures have got better the older he gets. In 2021, he recorded his best ever bowling figures for Lancashire – 7 for 19 – and in 2022, he took 36 Test match wickets, at an average of 19.8 runs – outstanding!

Whilst England fans chant "Oh Jimmy, Jimmy! Jimmy, Jimmy, Jimmy, Jimmy Anderson!" every time he bowls the ball, opponents are in awe of his skill and fitness. As for Jimmy himself, he reckons:

> **"As long as I am fit, contributing to the team and bowling well, then who knows how long I can go on for? Maybe 50 is a stretch but we will see!"**
>
> – Jimmy Anderson

Good Luck, Bad Luck

Cricketers can be a superstitious lot. Here are just a few of the strangest beliefs and rituals dreamt up by players and followers . . .

No-go numbers

In Australia, the number 87 is thought of as bad luck: an unlucky 13 short of a hundred. In England, the number 111, known as Nelson, is considered bad luck. So is double Nelson (222) and triple Nelson (333).

No one is certain where the superstition comes from, but it is common in local cricket in England, possibly because 111 looks like three stumps without the bails on top! The name Nelson may possibly come from a New Zealand team called Nelson. They played their first first-class cricket match in 1874 and scored 111. The team finished playing in 1891, when their last ever innings score was – you've guessed it – 111 again. Freaky!

Famous umpire David Shepherd used to be seen hopping from foot to foot when a team's score reached 111, 222 or 333. "When I was kid playing village cricket down in Devon," he explained.

"We found the only way to counteract something bad happening on a Nelson number was to get your feet off the ground . . . If I was on the field of play I would jump or hop."

David Shepherd

Individual players have superstitions too – even tough cookies like former Australian captain Steve Waugh. He always batted with the same red handkerchief in his pocket, given to him by his grandparents. Shubham Gill also carries a red hankie for luck, whilst West Indian all-rounder Andre Russell always taps his bat four times on the ground before facing every ball.

A kiss for luck

Sri Lankan bowler Lasith Malinga used to kiss the ball every time he ran in to bowl. Bearing in mind he bowled more than 18,000 balls for Sri Lanka and over 20,000 more for club teams, that's a lot of kisses!

Wash it lucky

Australia's Meg Lanning likes to sit in the corner of a dressing room before a game – a seat anywhere else will not do. Meg's teammate Jess Jonassen washes all the clothes she wears when she plays well and her team wins, so she can wear the exact same outfit in the next match.

Getting it right . . . or left?

Even the great Ellyse Perry has a superstition, always putting her right sock, shoe and pads on first. Indian legend Rahul Dravid also insisted on putting on his right pad first, whilst his teammate Sachin Tendulkar plumped for the left pad first every time.

Look out for more fun-filled books from Farshore!

Incredible Sports

Amazing Facts

Amazing Football Facts

INCREDIBLE RUGBY

60 TRUE STORIES
EVERY FAN NEEDS TO KNOW

INCREDIBLE GOLF

60 TRUE STORIES
EVERY FAN NEEDS TO KNOW

AMAZING FACTS

EVERY **8** YEAR OLD

NEEDS TO KNOW

AMAZING FACTS

EVERY **9** YEAR OLD

NEEDS TO KNOW

AMAZING FACTS

EVERY **10** YEAR OLD

NEEDS TO KNOW

AMAZING FOOTBALL FACTS

EVERY **8** YEAR OLD

NEEDS TO KNOW

AMAZING FOOTBALL FACTS

EVERY **9** YEAR OLD

NEEDS TO KNOW

AMAZING FOOTBALL FACTS

EVERY **10** YEAR OLD

NEEDS TO KNOW

CLIVE GIFFORD is an award-winning author of more than 200 books, including the official guide to the ICC Cricket World Cup 2019. His books have won the Blue Peter Children's Book Award, the Royal Society Young People's Book Prize, the School Library Association's Information Book Award and Smithsonian Museum's Notable Books For Children. Clive's played golf on three continents and once miss-hit a shot that bounced over Seve Ballesteros's car, just missing it!

LU ANDRADE is an illustrator from Ecuador, currently living in the mountains of Quito. She has studied everything from cinematography to graphic design. After focusing on digital animation for four years, she turned her hand to illustration, working on projects including *Good Night Stories for Rebel Girls*.